# So you want to be an

## ANCIENT EGYPTIAN PRINCESS?

Written by
Jacqueline Morley

Illustrated by
Nicholas Hewetson

Twenty-First Century Books
Brookfield, Connecticut

# Applying for the job

To create a good impression, your letter should be written in the ancient Egyptian way. They write on a kind of paper made from mashed and dried papyrus reed and use a reed pen and cakes of black and red paint. The ancient Egyptians invented paper while their neighbors were still writing by making marks in wet clay.

You should sit on the floor cross-legged, with the roll of papyrus on your knee. Write from right to left and start each new paragraph in red.

You will need some help because the ancient Egyptians write hieroglyphs (picture signs that sometimes stood for sounds and sometimes for whole words) so writing is quite complicated.

Most ordinary Egyptians do not learn to read and write, but princesses do. So you must get it right!

# Contents

# What applicants should know

Be prepared for a lengthy time journey – to more than 3,000 years ago. Yet even in those distant times, ancient Egypt already had a long history behind it. The map shows you your destination, in the northeastern corner of Africa. Notice how the River Nile flows the whole length of the land. A strip on either side of the river is lush and green while all the rest is desert. This is because in those days the river flooded each year, watering the nearby land and coating it with thick black mud. The ancient Egyptians believed this flood was a gift from the gods. It made the soil fertile so that crops grew plentifully and the country was rich. The wealth was very unevenly distributed. Most of it went to the ruling pharaoh, but since the ancient Egyptians thought their pharaohs came from the gods, they did not dream of complaining.

## Ancient Egypt

Giza
Memphis
EASTERN DESERT
WESTERN DESERT
RED SEA
Abydos
Valley of the Kings
RIVER NILE

# *Your new workplace*

S uppose that this morning you woke up in a palace – an ancient Egyptian palace of more than 3,000 years ago. You have servants to wait on you, and when you go out they follow you, carrying your sandals and waving tall fans of ostrich plumes to protect you from the fierce Egyptian sun. Inside the palace it is cool. The walls of its great reception halls are painted with garlands of flowers and birds; the starry ceilings rest on pillars shaped like lotus stems. Here your father the Pharaoh receives his ministers and guests. Beyond are the smaller rooms in which he lives. You do not enter these unless your father sends for you.

## *Royal family*

Pharaoh

Queen

## *In the palace garden*

Imagine yourself in a leafy garden, with palm trees and a refreshing pool. Only very rich people have gardens like this. Beyond the garden walls lies the city – hot, dusty, and crowded.

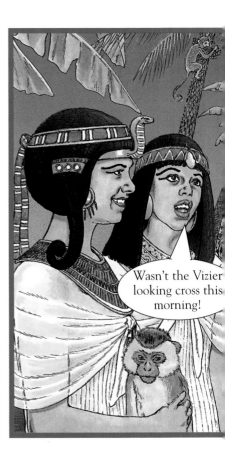

Wasn't the Vizier looking cross this morning!

You will have to get used to the idea that your father is a god. Everyone believes that each pharaoh is Horus, the son of Re the sun god. But pharaohs are human, and when he has time, your father enjoys family life.

## Lots of leisure time

You often go to the garden to talk with your mother, the Queen. As it is not customary for queens to take an active part in government, she spends quite a lot of time there.

We should be careful. He may be plotting something.

Here (right), with his secretary and fan-bearer, is your father's chief minister, the Vizier, who visits the palace daily. All other ministers report to him and he advises the Pharaoh. He might even have a say in choosing a husband for you.

## People you meet in the palace

Master of the household

Chief of palace guard

Head cook

Hundreds of servants work in the palace. Above are some of the most important ones.

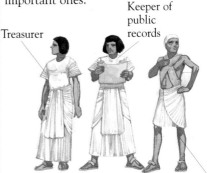

Treasurer

Keeper of public records

Commander of the army

These are some of the ministers who keep your father's government running smoothly. In theory, he does everything himself, since he is a god, but in practice they do all the hard work.

Secretary

Vizier

Fan-bearer

7

# Getting along with the rest of the team

You live in the women's part of the palace with all your father's wives and daughters, so you have to keep on good terms with them. It is normal for a pharaoh to have several wives, though most of his subjects have just one. Your mother is the chief wife, the only one with the title of Queen, so you are the "Great Royal Daughter." Your little brother is heir to the throne but there are quite a few wives with sons who are older. This can lead to jealousy and scheming. If anything happened to your father a cunning wife might try to get her son made pharaoh. It would help her plans if she could get him married to you, the Great Royal Daughter. It is not unusual for a pharaoh to marry his sister or half-sister.

Royal wife with children.

## Brothers and sisters galore

You are never short of company in the women's quarters. The royal sons are also brought up there until they are about nine, and there are lots of servants.

Did you win again, you clever boy? You are a marvel!

I'm sure his mother bribes her to say things like that.

## Royal babies

Women who have breast-milk (because they have just had a baby) are hired to breast-feed the royal babies.

## Ambitious wives

This wife is very artful. She wants to make her son the Pharaoh's favorite.

## Your room in the palace

The room you sleep in has painted walls and a small window, high up to keep out the sun's glare. The room may seem bare since the ancient Egyptians did not have all the types of furniture you are used to. They had beds, low tables, chairs, and stools. Instead of wardrobes they had storage boxes. Poor people slept on mats and had a few all-purpose stools.

A royal chair, of ebony inlaid with ivory and gold, has been made especially for you. It is a smaller version of the chairs your parents use.

Chair

Folding bed

You sleep in a bed like this, with a mattress and linen sheets. Your head goes at the plain end, your feet toward the footboard. You also have a carved stool in your room.

Stool

Instead of a pillow, you sleep with a headrest. It raises your head to keep it cool and clear of any creepy-crawlies.

## Your pets

Greyhound

Cat

Monkey

Keeping a monkey under control is a job for the servants.

Headrest

Toys

9

# Clothes for the job

*D*eciding what to wear is no problem in ancient Egypt. Every day you wear the same thing – a tunic of gauzy white linen over a body-hugging white sheath-dress. (Ancient Egyptian fashion never changed. Details varied over the centuries, but so gradually that no one noticed.) All women and young girls dress like this. Those who have to do hard work wear the sheath-dress by itself, and small children often go naked. Though the ladies of the court wear clothes like yours, it will still be easy to see you are a princess. The linen you wear is the finest possible. It takes a weaver nine months to make enough for one tunic, and you have hundreds of tunics.

Like most elegant people you have your head shaved and wear a wig. The best wigs are made of human hair; the worst are of date-palm fiber – they don't look so good!

## Ready to face the day

You would not be seen in public without eye makeup. Men and women wear it. It comes as pots of powdered mineral – green (from malachite) and gray (from galena).

For an official ceremony, put on grand jewelery, like this pendant of gold and semi-precious stones.

Wide bead collars are very popular. Yours are made of gold, coral, or turquoise.

That gray line is much too dark. Did you mix enough oil with it?

The beetle on this armband symbolizes the sun god. Most jewelery has some powerful symbol to ward off evil spirits.

## A well-groomed princess

A lotus bud, tucked in the headband, is worn for parties.

Greenish-blue eye shadow is made from malachite mixed with oil.

Wigs for special occasions have ringlets or braids.

Some people chew honey pills to sweeten their breath.

Everyday wigs are simpler.

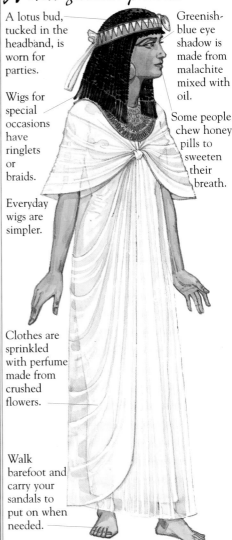

Clothes are sprinkled with perfume made from crushed flowers.

Walk barefoot and carry your sandals to put on when needed.

A servant helps you to dress in the morning and whenever you want to change. (The ancient Egyptians always look spotless – even those who do their own laundry, which means handwashing in the river.) It helps to have someone to arrange the folds of your wide tunic, which has to be gathered in and knotted at the chest.

11

# The working day

The first job of the day is to get washed, dressed, beautified (this takes quite a while) and perhaps visit your mother. Sometimes the Pharaoh sends word that he would like to see you before his official day begins. Then it is study time. A tutor teaches all the royal daughters together.

In the afternoon there is usually some ceremony to attend – an ambassador has to be welcomed, or a new provincial governor is presented with his seal of office. Often the event goes on into the evening and ends with a feast. But the best evenings are those that the Pharaoh spends alone with his favorite wife and children. That includes you!

## Lessons

A tutor reads aloud the words of respected authors of long ago. The pupil has to repeat them and write them from memory. Most lessons are like this.

## Carrying out official duties

Your official duties are limited to taking part in court ceremonies.

You stand near the throne while your father receives important visitors.

Greetings from far away, great Pharaoh.

Attending ceremonial events like this is the only part you play in matters of state. If you had been the eldest prince, by now your tutors would have been training you to govern, but princesses are not expected to rule.

# Behaving like a goddess

When your father gives a banquet, you must appear and eat with the guests.

Remember to be dignified. You must always act like the daughter of a god.

They must have come from *very* far away – their clothes are so odd.

In ancient Egypt it is taken for granted that men do all the professional work. Women are expected to look after the home. Poorer women have to work hard. They help grow the family's food, make things, and sell them in the markets.

# Cleanliness is next to godliness

Every morning you take a shower. You kneel in a trough and have water poured over you. Everyone washes daily, though there is no plumbing. They fetch water from wells or the Nile.

The ancient Egyptians are most particular about smelling clean and sweet. You are careful to shave every hair off your body. Then you rub yourself all over with scented oil.

Your attendant brings you a freshly laundered tunic. This one has hundreds of fine pleats, which have taken someone hours to put in with a pleating board. When you are ready you ask your servant how you look. There are no full-length mirrors.

13

# The right style for the job

To make a success of your job you must behave as young people are expected to in ancient Egypt. They have to be obedient and respectful. Long ago, so people believe, the gods ruled on earth and set things in order. The way people live now is just as the gods planned it then, so it is impossible to criticize the way things are done. If an older person tells you to do something, do not argue. Do not give an opinion unless asked and never contradict. These rules do not stop the ancient Egyptians from enjoying life. They never miss a chance to celebrate, and often joke about their betters behind their backs.

Professional performers, often women, provide the music for a feast. This trio plays the lute, the flute, and the zither.

## How to behave at a feast

Young people should not stare at other guests, push themselves forward, or take food before their elders have helped themselves.

The Vizier's in a better mood now. I wonder why?

At the start of the feast a servant will offer you a cone of scented wax for your head. The melting wax trickles down your face and wig and keeps you fresh all evening. Musicians play throughout the meal to entertain the guests.

## What sort of table manners are correct?

Don't worry about table manners. You do not eat at a table. People sit on low chairs or on mats. It is perfectly polite to eat with your fingers.

More wine! Let me drink to the health of your ka. (What is a ka? See page 28)

You do not have to be prim and proper for long. At first everyone is most polite. The Pharaoh and Queen have the seats of honor; you are the most important of the young ones. But soon people loosen up and start laughing and calling for wine.

## Food for a feast

A menu for a feast:
Bread in fancy
   shapes
Barley porridge
Roast fish
Pigeon stew
Roast quail
Spit-grilled kidney
Ribs of beef
Stewed figs
Honey cakes
Cheese
Lots of wine

The food is put out on low stands beside the guests, who help themselves. When everyone is full and feeling contented, entertainers give an acrobatic dancing display. The dancing is very lively, with amazing leaps and twists.

# How will you be paid?

You would expect a princess to get lots of pocket money but, in fact, no one in ancient Egypt gets any. You have gone so far back in time that money has not been thought of yet. Instead of using coins, people do their shopping by exchanging things that seem to them to be of equal value: three fresh fish and a wooden bowl for a pair of sandals, for example. This method is called bartering. As the daughter of the Pharaoh you can afford anything you want. The Pharaoh is immensely rich, for he owns everything in Egypt. He can order his subjects to erect vast buildings for him and fill them with precious objects.

Everything the palace uses is made or grown on the royal estates, but ordinary people have to shop for what they need. There are no big shops in ancient Egypt, only market stalls. This woman is offering a bead necklace to pay for some fruit.

## A visit to the royal workshops

All the furniture inlaid with ivory and gold, the painted and gilded statues, and the precious vessels supplied to the palace are made in the royal workshops.

## Jewelery

Don't expect glittering diamonds and sapphires. These cannot be obtained in ancient Egypt. Instead, jewelers get rich effects from semi-precious stones: amethyst, carnelian, jasper, turquoise, and deep-blue lapis lazuli.

# Ordering a new ring

Your splendid royal jewelery will be made in the workshops. Don't worry about paying. The craftsmen get a salary in the form of food and fine linen cloth.

It's the carving that matters. That sign of Horus will keep you safe, even from the Vizier's plots.

Most fine jewelery is set in gold, which comes from mines in the desert east of the Nile. Silver has to be imported from other countries, so it is more highly prized than gold and only used for the most precious work.

# Craftsmen in metal and stone

The royal craftsmen work to the highest standards. Overseers check each stage of the work, which follows long-established designs. Painters and sculptors are not expected to have new ideas or produce anything unusual. As always in ancient Egypt, the old ways of doing things are thought to be the best.

Coppersmiths smelting ore. To get the fire hot enough, a man works the bellows with his feet.

The skills of ancient Egyptian goldsmiths are famous far and wide. The two on the right are pouring molten gold into a mold to shape it. Those below are hammering sheet-gold into shape over blocks of wood.

This man is making a vase from porphyry, a very hard stone. He hollows it out with a drill weighted with stones so it turns evenly.

# Are there opportunities for travel?

The Pharaoh often leaves his capital, Memphis, to check on how more distant parts of his kingdom are being run. This means taking a journey along the Nile. Travel by river is by far the best way of getting around, since all important places are near it. Nobody can live far from the river. Beyond the fertile strip that its waters create there is nothing but desert. Privileged members of the Pharaoh's family and court go traveling with him. He likes to take his favorite wife and daughter, so you enjoy many river trips.

The pharaoh visits every province and listens to petitions from local people. His subjects have the right to appeal to him to judge their case if they feel that the court in their hometown has been unfair to them.

18

## The Nile: Egypt's highway

All sorts of boats use the river: big trading vessels bringing goods from afar; little fishing boats, homemade from papyrus reeds; pleasure boats, too.

Look, a falcon in the sky! A sign that Horus is protecting us.

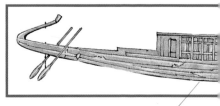

Royal barge

## Watching the banks slip by

You glide past villages and temples and wonder at the enormous pyramids. These are royal tombs of long ago, built many centuries before your father's time.

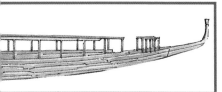

## Life by the river

Without the Nile the land would be desert, for it hardly ever rains. As the annual flood retreats it leaves water in a network of canals that criss-cross the countryside. These are constantly repaired to keep them watertight, since their water must last the farmers until the following year.

As you float along under your boat's shady canopy, you see many people busy in the fields. It is a hard life for most of them. Except in rare years when the flood fails, the harvest is always good, but farmers are allowed to keep only a tiny proportion of the crops they grow. Their own little patches of land are actually rented from some landowner, and as rent they have to farm his fields for him. On top of this, part of their own crop must be paid to the Pharaoh as tax.

Buckets hanging from poles, with a counterweight at the other end, are a common sight along the river. They are used to raise water for the fields. The farmer pulls on a rope to dip the empty bucket in the river or canal. The counterweight raises the full bucket.

# Extra duties

The noble ladies of ancient Egypt serve as priestesses in the temples. Do not be alarmed – you will not have many duties and it is considered a great honor to perform them.

Egypt is full of temples. Each town has at least one, and in the cities you will see many enormous ones. The ancient Egyptians are very religious. They do not honor the gods only on holy days. They take them into account in every decision they make in their daily lives.

The image of a god is kept in the innermost part of its temple. On holy days it is paraded through the streets, always covered, because it is too sacred to be seen by ordinary people. Priests dress the image and give it food daily, as if it were alive.

## Inside a temple

The gate leading to the temple opens onto a courtyard where townspeople leave offerings for the gods. They are not allowed to enter the temple itself. Only priests and priestesses may do so.

Temples have massive stone walls decorated with carved and painted scenes.

# Making music for the gods

As a priestess you join in the sacred dancing in the vast pillared hall of the temple and make music with a systrum, a sort of rattle that you shake. On holy days you are in the gods' procession.

When the musicians start, count to three and shake your systrum in time with me.

Tall obelisks, inscribed with hieroglyphs, flank the entrance gate.

# Gods and goddesses

You may think these gods seem rather fierce and odd, but to the ancient Egyptians they look just as they should. They expect gods to look stern and dignified and to display their special qualities in their appearance. Hathor, for instance, a loving goddess, has the head of a cow because she overflows with the milk of kindness. She often has a cow's body, too. Horus has a falcon's head because, like the falcon, he is supposed to be the eye of the sun.

 Hathor

 Horus

 Isis

Maat

Harakhty

Osiris

 Atum

 Khons

 Geb

21

# Are there any drawbacks?

A life of luxury in a land of sunshine – what could be better? Well, there are disadvantages to life in ancient Egypt. Sandstorms, for example, that blow from the desert. The sand gets everywhere – a palace is no protection! It gets into the cooking so that your teeth get worn down chewing on it; it inflames your eyes and fills your throat. No wonder people say that the desert is the home of demons. They get blamed for all misfortunes that have no obvious cause. This has results that you might find alarming. If you fall seriously ill the doctor will trust to amulets and spells to drive the evil spirits away.

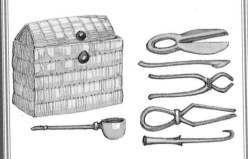

When the doctor arrives he may be carrying an instrument case made of cane and papyrus, like this one. It contains tools for performing operations.

## A visit from the doctor

The doctor gives you an herb mixture and says a spell to put you right.

Plenty of rest, a simple diet, and spells three times a day for you.

You may get bad chest problems from breathing sand into your lungs during sandstorms.

## Dangers to look out for

Nasties you may meet include crocodiles and scorpions.

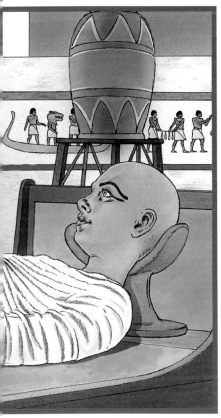

## When you are ill

Doctors can do a lot for you if you are unwell. They can set broken bones and treat burns. They know a great deal about how the body works and they understand the importance of diet. But they do not know about the existence of germs and cannot treat serious diseases. If you are very ill, people will suggest you ask a famous healer of long ago for help. Statues are put up in their memory, like this one of a woman healer. You must place offerings in front of the statue and beg the healer to cure you.

The eye of Horus, shown on this amulet, is a very powerful charm against evil.

You may have to watch people starve if locusts arrive. These insects land in swarms on crops and eat them up.

# Promotion — becoming Queen

As the Great Royal Daughter, you are likely to be the next pharaoh's queen. The much loved god Osiris married his sister Isis, so it is a god-like act for a pharaoh to marry his sister. Not all pharaohs do so, and their subjects do not copy the customs of the gods. When you are Queen you will have to hold court and attend long public ceremonies at the Pharaoh's side. You must also be tactful with the other wives.

In ancient Egypt people attach great importance to having their tomb ready and waiting for them, painted with scenes that have magical meanings. A queen needs a most magnificent one, and you give orders to your tomb painter.

## A royal ceremony

As Queen you help the Pharaoh to perform the ceremony of gold throwing.

When the Pharaoh wishes to honor someone who has served him well, he gives them gold.

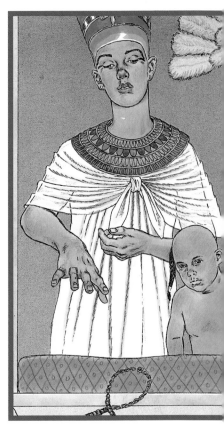

The ceremony is performed from a balcony of the palace, and the royal children give a helping hand. A great crowd gathers in the courtyard below and cheers as the gifts shower down – lots of gold collars, rings, and armbands.

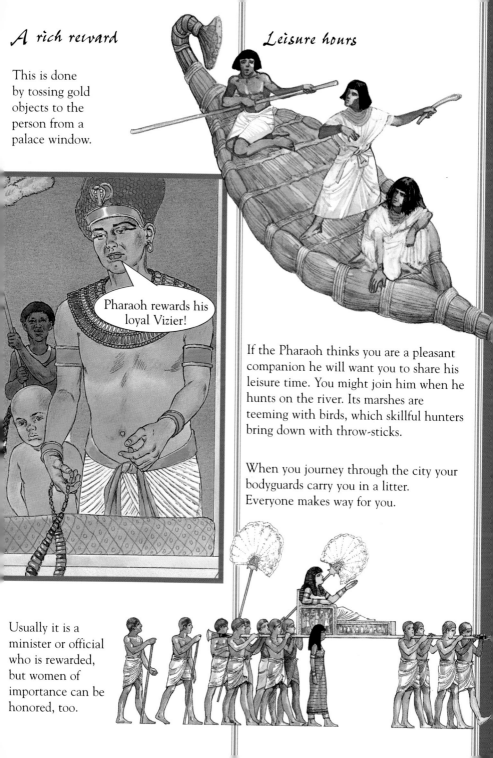

## A rich reward

This is done by tossing gold objects to the person from a palace window.

## Leisure hours

Pharaoh rewards his loyal Vizier!

If the Pharaoh thinks you are a pleasant companion he will want you to share his leisure time. You might join him when he hunts on the river. Its marshes are teeming with birds, which skillful hunters bring down with throw-sticks.

When you journey through the city your bodyguards carry you in a litter. Everyone makes way for you.

Usually it is a minister or official who is rewarded, but women of importance can be honored, too.

# Could you land the top job?

Your chances of becoming Pharaoh are slim. Even if a pharaoh has no sons, a daughter is not in line for the throne. There have been women rulers, but very few. One or two queens are known to have reigned briefly in troubled times when there was no clear heir. Only Queen Hatshepsut is known to have seized the throne and held on to it. She became regent in 1503 BC when her husband died, since the next Pharaoh was still a child. She would not give up power when he grew up, and so reigned as Pharaoh for more than twenty years, until her death.

Suppose by chance you have become Pharaoh. Remember that the existence of Egypt depends on you alone. Your rule must please the gods or they will not send the flood that makes things grow.

## Pharaoh at last

Here you are, seated on the throne of Horus. Your subjects believe that the gods have put you there, for everything happens exactly as the gods wish.

Your command is law and is written down as you speak. You know everything. You are chief judge in every court, chief priest of every temple, the maker of all decisions in government. Your ministers and priests are merely tools you use.

## Ruling in glory

A circlet like a serpent rings your forehead. The serpent's rearing head represents the sun god. Like the flame-spitting sun, you scorch your enemies.

She looks as though she means to stay there.

## Going to war

You are head of the army and must inspect your regiments. These are formed of archers, foot soldiers like this one, and officers in chariots. As Pharaoh, you must lead the way in battle, shooting arrows from your chariot as you hurtle toward the enemy.

Being a god, you cannot lose the battle (or if you do, you make sure the news is kept quiet). Hatshepsut did not lead her army personally, so if the idea alarms you perhaps you can get out of it.

Hatshepsut is shown here as a sphinx, wearing the false beard which is one of the emblems of a pharaoh.

# What are the long-term prospects?

You ou can look forward to the future with confidence. If the proper preparations have been made, you will live forever – not in this world, of course, but in the Land of the Dead, a pleasant place ruled by the god Osiris. It has a river and fields of golden corn, just like Egypt but without any work or worry. However, you will not get there unless an invisible part of you called your "ka" is kept alive. Everyone has a ka. Though it is a spirit, it needs a body to live in. So when you are dead your body must be preserved, to make it last forever. Then it will be sealed in your tomb, to provide a home for your ka.

Your body will be made into a mummy and put on a boat-shaped bier. Mourners will ferry it over the Nile to the tomb you had prepared for it on the western bank.

## A royal burial

This is your mummy in its case. Its lid (bottom right) bears your portrait.

I know we have to do t job properly for a roya mummy, but this Anub mask makes it hot wor

To ensure that you will be able to speak and eat in the next world, a ceremony called the Opening of the Mouth is held. Priests burn incense and touch the mouth on your mummy case with sacred objects.

Your body is now safely packaged, but next you must enter the Hall of Judgment where your heart is weighed by the jackal-headed god Anubis. Maat, goddess of truth, is watching and Thoth, god of writing, waits to note the result. If your heart is as light as the Feather of Truth in the other scale, all is well. A monster waits to gobble the heavy hearts of wicked people.

Your body has been drying out in natron (a sort of soda) for many weeks, to stop it from rotting. The embalmers have packed it with spices to keep it sweet. Now they are wrapping it in layers of linen, with amulets between them, to protect you.

# Your interview

Answer these questions to test your knowledge, then look at the opposite page to find out if you have the job.

Q1 How many wives does your father have?
A  As many as he likes.
B  One.
C  None.

Q2 What is put on your head at a feast?
A  A lump of wax.
B  A sun hat.
C  Plaits.

Q3 What is the best way to travel in ancient Egypt?
A  On foot.
B  On a camel.
C  In a boat.

Q4 What does the Pharaoh throw from his balcony?
A  His rubbish.
B  His gold.
C  His children.

Q5 What does the Pharaoh wear as a sign of kingship?
A  A false nose.
B  A false beard.
C  False eyelashes.

Q6 What must your heart be like to enter the Land of the Dead?
A  As light as a feather.
B  As heavy as lead.
C  As black as night.

Q7 When is the ceremony of the Opening of the Mouth performed?
A  When you are hungry.
B  When you are very bored.
C  When you are dead.

Q8 Ka is the name of what?
A  Your brother.
B  Your spirit.
C  Your favorite soft-drink.

# Glossary

**Amulet** Small decorative object, worn or carried, which was thought to ward off evil.

**Bier** Movable coffin stand.

**Carnelian** Red, semi-precious stone.

**Galena** Lead ore.

**Gilded** Covered with a layer of gold.

**Jasper** Red or yellow semi-precious stone.

**Lapis lazuli** Dark-blue semi-precious stone.

**Linen** Fabric woven from the fibers of the flax plant.

**Litter** Seat with horizontal carrying poles, which bearers carried on their shoulders.

**Lotus** Nile water-lily.

**Malachite** A green mineral.

**Molten** Melted by heat.

**Obelisk** Four-sided tapering pillar of stone.

**Petition** To make an official request for help from someone in authority.

**Pleat** Flattened fold or crease in cloth.

**Province** Region or division of a country.

**Quail** Small bird related to the partridge.

**Scorpions** Creatures related to spiders, with a poisonous sting in their tail.

**Seal** Small object with an official sign cut into it. Used to stamp documents with proof of ownership, by pressing the seal into a blob of wax.

**Smelting** To extract metal from ore by melting.

**Steward** An official responsible for running a household or estate.

**Throw-stick** Length of wood shaped so that it can be hurled accurately at a moving target.